QUARANTINE
Reflections
ACROSS TWO WORLDS

NORA D. CLINTON

ARCHWAY
PUBLISHING

Archway Publishing books may be ordered through booksellers or by contacting:

Archway Publishing
1663 Liberty Drive
Bloomington, IN 47403
www.archwaypublishing.com
844-669-3957

ISBN: 978-1-4808-9598-0 (sc)
ISBN: 978-1-4808-9599-7 (e)

Library of Congress Control Number: 2020917647

Print information available on the last page.

Archway Publishing rev. date: 09/17/2020

To my son,

my sister,

and the children of tomorrow

Without freedom of thought, there can be no such thing as wisdom; and no such thing as public liberty, without freedom of speech; which is the right of every man, as far as by it, he does not hurt or control the right of another: and this is the only check it ought to suffer, and the only bounds it ought to know.

Benjamin Franklin, "Silence Dogood, No. 8, 9 July 1722"

CONTENTS

CHAPTER 1

Early Years

Why I Want to Visit Portugal

When I was a child, my grandfather was my best friend, although he was seventy years my senior. I grew up in a one-bedroom apartment. My parents slept in the living room, while I shared the bedroom with my grandparents. Despite indigence and totalitarian serfdom, I was surrounded by love and had limitless access to stories and wisdom.

My grandfather had been a respected director of an insurance company, aptly named Phoenix. The company had been owned by Mr. Narcisso Arie, who belonged to a prominent Jewish family in my hometown of Sofia, Bulgaria. Mr. Arie hired my grandfather and quickly recognized his promise as an intelligent, industrious, and loyal employee. The two men developed a close professional bond and a deep, time-honored friendship.

In the early 1940s, Mr. Arie immigrated to Lisbon, Portugal, which provided a safe haven to numerous refugees during World War II. Before departing Bulgaria, he appointed my grandfather to take charge of the business.

The communists then nationalized the company but needed experts to teach them basic skills at the state-owned insurance outfit. They hired my grandfather to manage this effort but soon ordered him to dismiss two employees for political reasons. Their crime was "harboring ill musings toward the government." My grandfather refused to fire the employees on political grounds. And he disappeared overnight.

In those days, any individuals who expressed the slightest disagreement with the party line or posed even an imaginary threat by being educated or playing Western music—among many other "transgressions"—ran the risk of being kidnapped by state security and tortured. They were then sent to a correctional labor facility—a forced-labor prison for the extermination of perceived enemies of the people, better known as a gulag camp.

My grandmother went from door to door, imploring newly successful government members, who used to seek her husband's aid when they were down and out, to give her any news about his fate. At last, after several months of falling on deaf ears, she had a stroke of luck: one high-level official promised to find out his whereabouts. "I knew this was going to happen," he warned my grandmother. "Your husband is a good comrade, but unfortunately, he is a humanist."

The official kept his promise and learned that my grandfather was in a gulag camp south of the capital, called Bogdanov Dol. It was one of the most brutal camps in Bulgaria, if such a comparison is even possible where human suffering is concerned. My grandmother enlisted the assistance of a dauntless attorney, who discovered such a glaring and damning error of incompetence in the internment papers that my grandfather had to be released—an unheard-of occurrence of communists admitting fault.

His life had been spared, but he was never allowed to work again—a highly skilled expert in his prime with so much to contribute. My grandmother, who had been a devoted homemaker and a gracious hostess of sophisticated dinners, had to wake up before five each morning and sell trinkets at a kiosk in order to put basic food on the table.

Yet there was light in the tunnel—the couple was soon blessed with the birth of my mother, their only offspring after decades of childlessness. My grandparents lacked money for a baby pram, but a compassionate relative donated one. For nearly twenty years, things were calm, and life went on, as long as they knew to keep their thoughts private.

In 1968, the comrades' tanks invaded Prague, and my grandfather vanished again. An informant sitting at a café had recorded his conversation with a friend, in which both men expressed disapproval of the invasion. The government exiled my grandfather to an isolated, poverty-stricken village in northeast Bulgaria for one year, without permission to see his family. He was denied the simple joy of attending his daughter's high school graduation.

Fast-forward some ten years, and there I was, playing at home one gorgeous summer afternoon, when the doorbell rang. We did not have a telephone; visitors merely dropped by. Phones, cars, apartments, and other essential possessions were a privilege—people had to deserve them. They often waited five, ten, twenty, or more years to obtain them.

I opened the door and saw a kind, elderly man. He wore an elegant linen suit and looked foreign, but he addressed me in perfect Bulgarian. "My name is Narcisso Arie. I am an old friend of your grandfather's. Is he home? I sent him a letter that I was about to visit Sofia." The communist authorities opened and read personal mail and regularly decided not to deliver it, especially when it originated from the West.

"Please come in." I smiled. "I know who you are—we have heard so much about you! Unfortunately, we never received your letter, and my grandparents are in the countryside." I offered Mr. Arie a cup of real coffee, a treat reserved for special occasions. (On ordinary days, my family drank chicory imitation coffee.) We had a cordial chat for several hours.

When my grandfather learned that he had missed the visit of his dear friend, he was heartbroken—one of the exceptionally rare times I saw him cry. He knew there wouldn't be another chance of a reunion—Bulgaria kept its population locked behind barbed wire, and even free-world citizens were seldom fortunate to enter and exit unobstructed.

A few months later, around Christmas, I received a card from Mr. Arie. He wrote how saddened he was to miss his old friend, but he was delighted to have made a new, very young friend in my person. We became pen pals, and I eagerly devoured the stories about his long and difficult life. After arriving in Portugal, he could not find a job, due to a heart condition listed in his medical record. Finally, a sympathetic doctor told a white lie, and Mr. Arie enjoyed a successful career, got married, had several children and even more grandchildren. He lived to be over ninety years old—not bad for someone with a heart condition. In his letters to me, he described Lisbon, the pastel-hued edifices, the

Fado music, the culinary delights, the hilltop panoramas, and the glimmering ocean. So, ever since, I have dreamed of visiting Portugal.

I will certainly do it someday.

My grandparents, ca. 1936

My mother, 1968   My parents, 1971

Kindergarten Crumbs

When I was five, I attended kindergarten. While some teachers were warm and humane, the communist directive mandated that children be indoctrinated and humiliated every step of the way. This would serve as an instructive preview early on of what was to come in adulthood.

We sang a song about the party being our one true mother. It went like this: "You love your mother, and she may be a very fine person, but she only cares about you and your sister. We all, however, have one true mother—the communist party that cares for us all."

One day, we were finishing up the usual morning snack, titled "people's bun." The kindergarten principal then proceeded to count how many crumbs each child had generated. My pals quickly gobbled up their crumbs. Being foolishly honest, I left mine as they were—a Goldilocks amount of crumbs, not too many, not too few. I was publicly shamed for having the most crumbs of the class.

My first day at school was no different. We were seated in alphabetical order and assigned numbers, to be referred to impersonally and not by our own names. I ended up next to a boy named Nicky, who impishly urged me to throw pebbles at the ostentatious ficus tree container near the teacher's desk.

The teacher happened to walk in that very instant, and she dragged us both by our ears and slapped our faces before the entire class. I started crying, which incensed her even more. "Why the tears?" she asked. "I didn't even hit you that hard."

As the only child of academic parents, I knew some big

words and had begun to read at the age of three. I looked her in the eyes and retorted, "I am not crying on account of physical pain but public humiliation." She was speechless.

In third grade, I was attending an extracurricular English class. The boy next to me, named Lucky, was about to be flunked and consequently beaten at home, so I tutored him and helped him get an A. In an innocent burst of joyous gratitude, he kissed me on the cheek. The next period, my regular desk-mate, Nicky, accused me of being "Lucky's mistress." He used a word that has the same derivation in Bulgarian as the English word "lover." I had no idea what mistress meant but vigorously denied the accusation.

The teacher walked in amid the heated argument. "What is going on here?"

"Comrade teacher," I responded, "Nicky accused me of being Lucky's mistress."

The teacher slapped my right cheek. "Do you know what that means?"

"Not exactly," I admitted. "But it shouldn't be that bad, since it derives from the word for love." Needless to say, I was then slapped on the left cheek, for symmetry and good measure.

Disgraced, Lucky and I left school together and walked hand in hand into the sunset—or so it seemed. He picked a velveteen-pink rose and gave it to me. We passed by a woman's dimly lit basement; she was Lucky's neighbor and was fashioning variegated pottery, which we admired from the minuscule window. "Is this your wife?" she benevolently teased Lucky.

"She sure is," he beamed proudly. I felt vindicated and fully convinced that love conquers all.

First Day at School, 1977

Radioactive Spinach

Few people in the West are aware that high school and college students, soldiers, and other groups were engaged in forced labor to help the unsustainable communist economy. They dug ditches, painted buildings, worked in the fields or can factories—the so-called "merry brigades."

A brigade supervisor once scolded me when I was fifteen, "You'll rest when you die!" I was taking a five-minute breather after strenuously digging with a pickaxe in the blazing June sun. One of my brigade locations was infested by poisonous snakes. Our teachers instructed us to wear two pairs of long woolen socks in the scorching summer heat, to ward off the snakes. Apparently it worked.

The Bulgarian authorities mentioned the news of Chernobyl in passing, as an innocuous mishap fully under control by the brotherly Soviet state. A major nuclear disaster was incompatible with the officially touted image of the Soviet Union as the most advanced and humane society, which made no mistakes. Chernobyl was still another painfully graphic example of the living hell that was the communist "paradise on Earth."

A few days after the explosion, my classmates and I were to collect spinach at a vast cooperative farm, after spring rains and gusts of wind had spread the radioactive cloud across great swaths of territory in many countries. Our principal called the Ministry of Health to inquire if this was safe. "We are talking about eighth-grade children," she pleaded. The ministry assured her there was no risk, and we gathered radioactive spinach from dawn to dusk, when a new order arrived from above: "Destroy the spinach!"

I then proceeded to a dinner party for a relative whose name-day we celebrated fondly each year. Name-day celebrations fall on the respective saint's holiday and are widespread in Christian Orthodox and Catholic countries. In those times, name-days were even more significant than birthdays. Everyone knew when it was someone's name-day, and the honoree had the heartwarming obligation to expect impromptu visitors arriving to pay their respects.

My extended family included a number of medical doctors, who were aghast upon learning that I had spent the day picking radioactive spinach. "You must take iodine," they urged me, "immediately!" They diluted some iodine in water and made me chug it. It left a burning sensation in my esophagus, but perhaps it saved my life.

The criminal negligence and intentional deception by communist governments caused countless Chernobyl-related deaths, some of whom were dear friends and classmates. Both the immediate and long-term impact of the disaster and its cover-up resulted in severely deformed, stunted, or dead forests, animals, and human beings, while the cancer incidence in the affected countries over the next couple of decades increased exponentially.

To this day, I abhor collectivism, group thinking, peer pressure, and any imposition over individual freedom of thought or expression. Imagine my delight when a few years ago, a good friend coined an immortal Latin maxim: *Etiam si omnes, ego non.* It sounds much better in Latin and means: "Even if all, I shall not."

My friend signed his emails with it, and I enthusiastically congratulated him on his brilliance and bravery. "Your words are music to my ears," I chuckled. "What prompted this?"

"My young son recently asked me if I was a community builder," my friend elaborated. "The very word 'community' gives me the creeps," he added. "After all I was raised by communists."

May we never lose the courage to think for ourselves and speak our conscience, even if all others ostracize us! Often this is easier said than done.

"Down with Article One!"

The Berlin Wall crumbled when I was in twelfth grade. We watched with a mixture of awe and disbelief how regular German citizens reclaimed their freedom, how they pierced the hitherto impenetrable Iron Curtain and ripped it to shreds. Even so, only a handful of people in Bulgaria dared to imagine we could soon be free. On November 10, 1989, I came home from school and boldly declared, "There are rumors that Zhivkov will resign today."

Zhivkov was our peasant-turned-king dictator, who had abused the country for thirty-six years. When he was prosecuted for his crimes, one excuse was he had saved Bulgaria unnecessary expenses by having his nurse darn his socks. The communist élite stole millions, secretly wired to Swiss banks, while delaying the transition to democracy as much as they could.

My parents glanced at me as if I had suffered a fit of temporary insanity, but curiosity prevailed, and we turned on the news. Sure enough, a coup was underway, and seemingly benign reformists replaced communist hardliners—a clever plot to hold on to political and economic power as long as possible, which exacerbated the ordinary misery and further depleted the limited goods' supply.

At that time, our school had student visitors from Italy, who were also in twelfth grade. We tried our best to conceal our poverty and regale them with proverbial Balkan hospitality. My family took a loan from relatives in order to show our guest as grand a time as possible. Even so, our Italian friends must have been so distressed by the disheartening sight of the shops' empty shelves that they sent us Christmas presents consisting of flour, sugar, and oil.

Bill Bryson vividly describes those times in his poignantly hilarious travel memoir, *Neither Here nor There*:

> I had read that things were desperate in Bulgaria—that people began lining up for milk at 4:30 in the morning, that the price of some staples had gone up 800 percent in a year, that the country had $10.8 billion of debt and so little money that there were only funds enough in the central bank to cover seven minutes' worth of imports— but nothing had prepared me for the sight of several hundred people queuing around the block just to buy a loaf of bread or a few ounces of scraggy meat.[1]

On December 14, 1989, I went to school as usual. Some teachers admonished us to avoid the anti-government rally that day, as rumors of violence began circulating. The Tiananmen Square massacre was still a fresh wound. Being reckless souls, we ignored the warning and gathered in front of the Bulgarian Parliament for a peaceful demonstration demanding removal of Article One of the Constitution, which effectively equated the communist party with the state and its governance. We wanted a multiparty system and free elections.

---

[1] Bill Bryson, *Neither here nor there: travels in Europe* (New York, NY: Perennial, 2001), 276.

"Down with Article One!" We chanted for hours. Finally the new state leader, the "benign reformist," growled to the minister of defense, "It is best if the tanks came." Due to the opposition's prudent appeal that we all disperse, no one was killed. Fortunately, an observer's video camera accidentally recorded the order to attack the nation's peacefully protesting citizens, many of whom were children, and after months of civil disobedience, the head of state had no viable choice but to resign.

I can still feel the warm, euphoric wave of kindness and humanity that permeated our rallies. We smilingly let each other pass by, even in the most crowded areas of the protests. We felt united by a rare sense of brotherhood and the palpable joy of freedom. I don't recall any vandalism, looting, or other violence fueled by provocateurs. We simply wanted to be heard and respected.

While we were a long way away from a true democracy, we felt elated and empowered that for the first time in our lives, we had made a difference as citizens and individuals. We embraced strangers on the streets and sang our newly composed, homegrown odes of joy and paeans to liberty, such as "Communism is Departing—Sweet Dreams, Children!" or "The Last Waltz." We were no longer dispensable, faceless cogs in the omnipotent totalitarian machine.

CHAPTER 2

Academic Pursuits

A Rainy Day in London

I graduated from Sofia University in the mid-nineties and was eager to continue my education and travel the world. An English-speaking country was a natural choice, as I had studied English since the age of six. Deprived of opportunities to speak it, I learned English passively, as if it were a dead language, the same way I approached Latin and Greek. I developed a sizable vocabulary and etymological expertise and understood Shakespeare's language but had no clue about elementary slang and colloquial expressions.

I had saved some money from doing translation work and giving private lessons, so I signed up for a summer English course in Luton, in order to acquire conversational proficiency. I had the pleasure to visit London for the first time and couldn't get enough of the city's mesmerizing sights and sounds. I sometimes walked ten hours a day to absorb as much as humanly possible.

During one such exploratory mission, I passed by the classics department at University College London. Suddenly, the refreshing drizzle, which had not deterred me from my stroll, turned into a downpour. I had no choice but to seek shelter inside the building, so I decided to make the best of it.

I entered the classics office, introduced myself, and informed the administrator that I had studied Greek and Latin for ten years and endeavored to deepen my knowledge. I must have exuded some inspired determination, since she gave me a welcoming smile and suggested, "Why don't you take a seat and wait a minute?"

A benevolent professor emerged and interviewed me about my educational background. After a five-minute heartfelt exchange, he invited me to apply to their master's program. I was accepted, graduated, and went on to pursue a doctorate in the United States after having the good fortune to win a highly competitive scholarship.

What a difference a rainy day makes, especially when one is young and open to turning lemons into lemonade!

Marveling at British Universities: Summer of 1994

A Ham-and-Cheese Sandwich, Please!

I arrived in Ithaca, New York, in August 1996 to do my doctorate. After what had seemed an interminable journey the day before, I awoke famished and sauntered around College Town in search of victuals. I came across a bohemian café named Stella's, frequented by bright-eyed students perusing tattered tomes, and ordered a ham-and-cheese sandwich. I had always considered a ham-and-cheese sandwich to be nothing more than what the name suggested.

Little did I know this would be a memorable paragon of free-market economy and a kaleidoscope of magical abundance. The server asked with a gentle smile, "What kind of bread would you like?"

I was confused. "What kind do you have?"

"White, wheat, rye, pumpernickel, pita, sprouted, flourless …" After I hesitantly chose, he continued, "Cheddar, provolone, brie, gouda, Havarti, pepper jack, or American?" Followed by, "Do you want mustard, mayo, butter, or cream cheese? Peppers, tomatoes, relish, onions, lettuce, arugula, or sprouts?" And to top it all off, "How about a pickle?"

I felt exhausted after ordering my first American sandwich, yet almost tearful with amazement and appreciation. For months afterward, I walked around the spacious grocery stores, just admiring all the colors, bright lights, and mind-boggling varieties of unimaginable delicacies.

I became a frequent visitor at College Town Bagels. One morning, a woman made a loud scene complaining that her cappuccino did not contain soy milk but skim milk instead. The server apologized profusely and offered her a free drink. The woman was merciless and demanded to speak with the manager. She continued to yell and disrupt the patrons' peaceful breakfast, so the manager finally advised her she was free to get her cappuccino elsewhere. The next day, I saw her with a placard in front of the coffee shop. She had assembled a meager crowd of acolytes, who boycotted and vilified the café for refusing to serve her. My first thought was, *Don't these people have real problems to worry about? What spoiled fools they are!*

Then it dawned on me: this is what it means to be acutely aware of one's rights and to have no fear of standing up for oneself. These sometimes asinine but often justified complaints are what keeps the system honest.

Celebrating my 2002 PhD graduation with my father:

Cornell campus, Commencement 2003

"Dangerous People" or the Value of Classical Education

Many years ago, my husband and I took a night train from Sofia to Athens. I love trains and savored the prospect of a romantic journey through picturesque snow-clad countryside. A first-class ticket in the sleeping car was just fifty dollars. We enjoyed the cozy, soporific ride, only to be abruptly awakened at midnight by a border guard who checked the passengers' passports. Bulgaria still had a communist-era regulation, whereby foreigners had to register with the police if they were guests at someone's home.

My husband had spent Christmas with my dear father and me, and the last thing I wanted to do was ruin his holiday by dragging him to a police station and waiting for hours just to register him as my guest. I apologized to the border guard and explained that we didn't get a chance to report to the police. I "repented" and promised this would never happen again.

The guard was unmoved by my contrition and demanded an enormous bribe—more than people made in a year. At that point, I objected. "If there is an officially determined fine, I would like to see proof of the amount." Of course, he could not produce proof. I kept insisting politely but firmly and threatened to check with the government what the fine was, if any. He realized I could get him in trouble and relented.

"What do you do for a living?" he demanded to know. I humbly explained I was a "classical philologist," as classicists were titled in Bulgaria. He slammed the door in frustration. "You classical philologists are dangerous people!" I felt almost proud to be called *dangerous* by a corrupt border official.

Joke aside, it is impossible to overestimate the value of a classical education. Churchill's rhetoric would not have been half as powerful if he didn't know his Cicero. Understanding Latin and Greek opened my eyes to the origins and true meaning of countless scholarly and scientific words in English and made complex terminology a breeze.

More importantly, a classical education teaches young minds that very little is new under the sun. It provides a measure of immunity against Orwellian temptations to impose a dehumanizing new order. A person intimately familiar with the ethos of Pericles's *Funeral Oration,* for instance, is less likely to fall prey to the soulless allure of a brave new world.

Of course, classical education is by no means the only way to remain impervious to utopias' siren calls; nor is it a bulletproof guarantee. Plain common sense and a simple ethical compass to navigate the turbulent maze of moral relativism will often suffice.

That is why millions of decent, hard-working people, uninitiated into intellectual snobbery, tend to be wiser judges of events and philosophies than erudite pundits.

Revisiting Greece in 2019: the majestic island of
Samothrace, where I worked for several summers
on a book of ancient documents on stone

"Great Spirits" versus "Useful Idiots"

I got my PhD and then my first job as a classics research
associate. It was a golden time: I got married, my son was
born, and I had an attractive job writing scholarly books
and articles and teaching classical languages. I was even
fortunate to co-establish a charitable foundation with my
husband and provide a modicum of help to my beloved
country of birth.

After the completion of my research appointment, whose
bliss had endured for seven years, I started applying for pro-
fessorial positions. I sent but a handful of applications, only
for opportunities that truly interested me. Although classics
departments had been somewhat spared from turning into
ideological conveyor belts promoting modernized Marxist

dogmas and penalizing dissenters, a growing contingent of classicists taught unproven subjective theories at the expense of good old-fashioned training in facts, documents, and languages. I had no passion for disseminating such theories, having published extensively in the field of ancient documents on stone.

Finally, a dream job opened up at Berkeley for a tenure-track professorship of epigraphy—the study of writing on hard surfaces. I was invited for an interview and then to deliver a lecture—a delightful experience in a breathtaking paradise on Earth, which beckoned, sun-kissed, luscious, and laid-back, even in January. I ended up being a runner-up for the job, which in retrospect was a blessing in disguise.

While my academic hosts wined and dined me as a promising job candidate, for which I felt most obliged, they invariably took me to the Freedom of Speech Café, where I received a powerful dose of anti-American sentiment. I love and admire America, and this made my blood boil. I politely underscored that freedom of speech was a privilege this country had continually enjoyed; if socialist intellectuals wanted to experience its real absence, they should relocate to a communist country.

How was I to resolve the irreconcilable dilemma between my passionate love for scholarship and my gut-wrenching disappointment with those American intellectuals who condoned communist crimes? My parents had been academics, and I had dreamed of becoming one myself since the age of six. At that age, I wrote my first "dissertation," which consisted of a title page; ten pages with educational illustrations

I meticulously drew and redrew, accompanied by detailed captions; and a judicious conclusion. The impetus had come from my beloved mother's PhD dissertation, which she defended at that time. Her example inspired me to produce a dissertation of my own, a term I childishly assumed derived from the word for *dessert,* since it served as the crowning achievement, the cherry on top of someone's doctorate.

I grew up with a profound sense of admiration for all those "great spirits," who, according to Einstein's prophetic adage, "always encountered violent opposition from mediocre minds." I felt incredibly blessed, at all academic institutions I attended, to have learned from such great spirits, who regarded facts as sacrosanct, while encouraging free thought and curiosity. To them I owe eternal thanks.

How different these honorable scholars and scientists were from the cookie-cutter proponents of pro-communist dogma and anti-American platitudes, who had replaced objective knowledge with ignorant propaganda. While constructive criticism of one's government stimulates democracy, the Marxist intellectuals at Western universities engage in a destructive rewriting of history that defies the principles of scholarship.

Were these the same duty-bound Americans in whom millions of Eastern Europeans placed their hope of deliverance—that they will "tear down this wall" one day, gallop in on white horses, and rescue us from Big Brother? In 1986, Ivailo Petrov published *Wolf Hunt*, a profound and intrepid portrayal of the communist persecution of Bulgarian peasants, who lost their land, livestock, livelihood, and often lives. One of the novel's main characters utters the wishful prophesy that the Americans will come: "If they don't come in our time, then they'll come in our children's or our grand-children's time. This world wasn't created yesterday, it has its way of doing things. What was again will be."[2] Among Bulgarian dissidents, these words assumed a life of their own, repeated from mouth to mouth—whispered at first, then timidly voiced, and at last boldly proclaimed.

My disillusionment with mainstream intelligentsia con-tinued to intensify. One professor I knew, who earned a six-figure salary, was an unabashed self-proclaimed commu-nist, who enjoyed a luxurious house with acres of majestic pines and an emerald pond. He incessantly directed invec-tives at the United States and sang "The Internationale" at his bon-vivant soirees, after distributing gaudy pink bro-chures with this dreadful anthem's lyrics to his unfortunate guests.

The French have fittingly labeled this phenomenon "left caviar" or "champagne socialism." Just think of George Bernard Shaw, who shamelessly propagated eugenics and genocide, offered to assist Hitler and Mussolini, and lauded Stalin's extermination camps as though they were a quaint holiday arrangement of voluntary duration.

Even more eloquent is the term "useful idiots," allegedly coined by Lenin to describe Western intellectuals and jour-nalists who were sympathetic to the communist regime, yet despised by its leadership for their naiveté, while being ruthlessly used by it to manipulate free-world media and impressionable young minds. I kept arguing with useful

---

[2] Ivailo Petrov, *Wolf Hunt*, trans. Angela Rodel (Brooklyn, NY: Archipelago Books, 2017), 118.

idiots, to the point of painful exasperation, and finally re-linquished a successful academic career, appalled by their hypocrisy and ingratitude.

My education and the noble minds who sought to impart their wisdom to me will always be a part of my soul. I never regretted my decision to bid farewell to academia, or rather, what has become of it, and set sail on uncharted seas that guided me to a new vocational harbor I now treasure every day—but let this be the subject of another book.

Visiting Berkeley and the Bay Area in January 2007

CHAPTER 3

Quarantine Reflections

Fast-forward to the spring of 2020 and its heart-rending loss of life and surreal self-imprisonment. Now, more than ever, the dichotomy between totalitarian dictatorships and free societies shines stunningly clear.

If China had been a free society, the heroic doctors who first warned about the contagion would not have been silenced and persecuted. The infection would have stayed limited to its original areas and efficiently contained, while the wider world would have remained largely unscathed. Instead, it was Chernobyl all over again—covering up the catastrophe and causing unnecessary sacrifice of human life in true communist fashion, then blaming it on the West and the United States in particular.

The essays that follow are the offspring of my quarantine reflections—I hope they serve as a rueful reminder to the young and those yet unborn why we always ought to choose freedom over tyranny.

A Bird's-Eye View

I can't stop thinking of a story about an old man from a secluded village who lost his eyesight shortly before his country was liberated from a centuries-long foreign domination.[3] He avidly imbibed the good news and each subsequent tale of newly found prosperity. Soon a railroad brought life to his forsaken corner.

Every day he stumbled toward the nearby cliff and greeted the train. He was perplexed by the political bickering of his neighbors, who possessed vision but were plagued by pusillanimous discontent. He rejoiced in his homeland's palpable independence and died with a smile, greeting the passing train.

I arrived in America some twenty years ago and became a grateful new citizen. Not a day passes without my counting my blessings. That is why I feel acute anguish when I witness severely distorted coverage of COVID-19 data. Having survived communism, I have a built-in radar for totalitarian deception.

Commending the Chinese government, which concealed the deadly dangers and persecuted whistleblowers, for its dubious success, harms myriad Chinese citizens who continue to suffer not only the disease's ravages but relentless oppression.

Comparing absolute numbers of COVID-19 cases without considering percentages of tested or total population is scientifically unsound, but truly disturbing is the clamoring

---

[3] The story is titled "Grandpa Yotso Sees," by Ivan Vazov, one of the most influential and acclaimed Bulgarian writers.

that America is the worst actor in this pandemic tragedy of innocent lives lost. It erodes our morale, precisely when we need confidence that the values we share far surpass what divides us.

We need a newcomer's bird's-eye view or the foresight of a blind man who could see what matters with his heart.

"The Good Fight"

Remember season three of *The Good Fight*? Prominent liberal attorney Diane Lockhart joins an underground antigovernment group, only to abandon them with revulsion when apprised of their terrorist tactics and Machiavellian ethics. Her dependable conservative husband, Kurt, risks all to save her, while she in turn, out of love, writes his career-pivotal speech, bestowing lavish accolade on a president she detests.

We all have our views, but our country's founding precepts, inherent integrity, and self-correcting mechanisms are more resilient than partisan politics, at least for the time being. *The Good Fight* admonishes us, with its artistic originality and incisive wit, that whether liberal or conservative, decent Americans would valiantly leap to each other's defense when challenged by left or right extremists alike.

The very terms *left* and *right* are notoriously misleading and do way more harm than good. They conjure up the image of an axis, with the alt-right and radical left as polar opposites. This couldn't be further from the truth.

Whether national or international, Nazi or communist, totalitarian socialism has the same criminal disregard for individual rights in favor of an all-powerful social entity. Both so-called left and right extremes have no place in the normal political spectrum. They belong on a completely different plane—a parallel universe composed of seemingly opposite, yet horridly akin, ideological malignancies, whose purpose is to obliterate Western democratic tradition and its historical values.

Allow me to make an analogy that may be hitting too close to home. Like a virus that keeps altering its strains, these ideologies have assumed the shape of communism, national socialism, ecoterrorism, Islamic terrorism, or cultural Marxism, to name just a few familiar mutations. Their common enemy is humanity's prosperity and liberty, particularly as exemplified by free democratic societies.

Understanding their shared nature and excising them from a healthy political organism by raising awareness of their destructive goals is the only effective inoculation against their chameleonic pervasiveness.

Thanos and the Avengers

My teenage son fell in love with *The Avengers* saga last summer. He insisted that we watch it all within a couple of days. At first I dreaded the idea, since my favorite films are contemplative, mellow, witty, and wise human-interest stories. I must confess, however, that the allegorical dimensions of this fast-paced modern epic were both impressive and fascinating. It teaches the young to differentiate between good and evil, heroes and villains—a refreshing and much-needed worldview against the backdrop of intellectual cynicism and moral relativism.

Take Thanos, for example. Concerned about population growth and limited resources, this unsightly champion of socialist utopia "saves" the world by randomly wiping out 50 percent of mankind. Is this some bizarre far-fetched fiction? Unfortunately not. Just think of all the followers of Thomas Malthus and their misguided lament for the "tragedy of the commons," a term whose original concept as intended by William Forster Lloyd, long before it was expressly formulated by Garret Hardin, is also frequently misunderstood to justify eugenics.

Population-control theories have intermittently flared up and are once again becoming alarmingly in vogue. Let us not forget that Nazis and communists were their macabre practitioners, who often used the concept of limited resources as an excuse for mass murder. Today the population-control virus has once again found a receptive host in radical environmentalism. I saw social media posts going viral, suggesting COVID-19 was nature's just punishment for man's actions. Some activists were deeply concerned about the rights of bats and dismissed loss of human life as an unfortunate but necessary population-control mechanism.

There are two kinds of environmentalists: those who care about people and those who despise them. Those who care about people long to see them able and flourishing in a beautiful, healthy environment. They welcome industrial advancement and employ ever-improving state-of-the-art technology to reduce pollution. They contribute their expertise with unassuming determination, just like Boyan Slat, who invented an ingenious ocean-cleaning system while he was just a teenage boy in the Netherlands.

Those environmentalists who despise people create an artificial opposition between man and nature, individual prosperity and a thriving society. They are proponents of what Churchill eloquently dubbed "the philosophy of failure, the creed of ignorance, and the gospel of envy, whose inherent virtue is the equal sharing of misery." Yes, we are talking about garden-variety misanthropic socialism.

Here it is crucial to make the following terminological distinction: socialism should not be confused with classical liberal ideology, which advocates better working conditions and life-improving measures. Classical liberalism is a healthy part of a normal political dialogue between stimulating economic advancement and caring for people's well-being. The difference between such liberal attitudes and socialism is humanism.

Classical liberals wish to improve the human condition, while socialists impose the abstract good of a social entity over the concrete good of human beings. The common denominator of radical environmentalism and totalitarian socialism is antihumanism—the devaluation of human prosperity, freedom, and ultimately life.

We need to lay bare the true underlying motives of totalitarian environmentalists and expel pathological anomalies from a sound political dialogue and practice. We need to apply apolitical, rigorous science to examine the current parameters of climate change, a complex phenomenon accompanying the Earth's existence since time immemorial. Freeman Dyson, for example, the widely respected free-spirited scientist and climate expert at the Institute for Advanced Study, who sadly passed away recently, always reminded young scientists to apply common sense, keep an inquisitive mind, and separate fact from cult.

Reducing pollution, protecting our planet, and safeguarding its spectacular splendor is a most worthy cause for the simple reason that it is *people's* home, *humanity's* only known abode. We need to practice good housekeeping for the sake of our health, longevity, and legacy—there is no more conflict of interest between mankind and its global habitat than between a family and its everyday home.

Promoting the narrative that Shakespeare's "beauty of the world" and "paragon of animals" is infinitely worse than any other animal, the planet's greatest enemy, a greedy rapist of its resources, who should give up the fruits of its ingenuity and sheepishly revel in preindustrial loincloth subsistence, is as preposterous as it is pernicious. What about Icarus and the human spirit's indomitable quest to conquer the skies? How can modern medicine save lives without the use of plastic? How can we deliver timely necessities without rapid transportation?

The only viable solution to poverty, pollution, and limited resources lies not in population control and extravagant government spending but in the never-ending innovations that keep improving the human condition. Is it a coincidence that America gave the world the electric bulb, washing machine, telegraph, airplane, surgical anesthesia, life-saving medical technology, computer, email, digital camera, space shuttle, cell phone, WiFi, and so many other inventions, without which we cannot imagine our charmed existence?

Life-improving innovations can never be born from the tortured apocalyptic vision of Thanos. They can only be the unapologetically glorious progeny of a free society.

The Greek King and the Potatoes

Legend has it that following Greece's independence in the 1820s, King Otto and Prime Minister Kapodistrias embarked on a mission to introduce Greek farmers to growing potatoes, in order to help the economy. Free piles of potatoes were left at the farmers' disposal throughout the country to be eventually replanted. The farmers assumed the potatoes were either worthless or there was a catch involved and wouldn't touch them with a ten-foot pole.

The government then placed armed guards around the free piles; the guards knew to turn a blind eye when the farmers secretly helped themselves to this strange new food. The potatoes had suddenly acquired value as something scarce and protected, and the piles rapidly vanished, which helped stave off the imminent hunger and poverty.

Similarly, receiving handouts is less beneficial than receiving motivation that heals a broken spirit and upholds a person's dignity. Anyone can fall on hard times and deserves compassionate understanding, but an attitude of entitlement promotes helplessness, while a dignified sense of personal responsibility frequently paves the way to a better fortune.

My husband and I have been managing a charity devoted to international education, cultural exchange, and American values. One of the best decisions we ever made was to employ a young man, who was earning a pittance at a dead-end job for an ungrateful miserly boss. His boss forbade him to leave his apartment for twelve hours a day—the young man was supposed to wait by his landline phone in case his boss might need him, though mobile phones were ubiquitous and reasonably priced. We recognized this man's capabilities and work ethic and gradually promoted him to a high management position. In short, he has been a godsend to our charity's operational needs.

As an unknown sage once remarked, "The best thing you could give someone is a chance."

Cassie Nightingale, Venus, and Mars

While surfing through the TV channels one relaxing evening, I stumbled across the Hallmark series *The Good Witch*—and was instantly intrigued. *The Good Witch* is not about New Age mysticism. It is a contemporary fairy tale about kindness and love. How did a simple story of helping one's neighbor become a rousing success with ever-growing numbers of fans, in our morally confused era that dismisses traditional behavior models?

Cassie Nightingale is a refreshing example of a woman's most enchanting qualities. She is feminine and caring, a loving mother and wife, yet an independent thinker and owner of two thriving businesses. She helps people without judgment and forgives those who hurt her without tolerating abuse. Men are irresistibly drawn to her inner beauty, and women naturally seek her friendship and advice.

The popularity of *The Good Witch* is a humbling lesson that we cannot escape our innate predispositions. While no person should *ever* be subjected to discrimination, disrespect, or ridicule on account of sexual orientation, this need not suggest that femininity and masculinity should become offensive, or at best, obsolete notions.

The fact that women could excel in traditionally male professions or vice versa, does not mean that gender differences are an artificial societal construct. These differences, though manifested in varying degrees and with unique flavors, are both beautiful and profound.

A few years ago, I attended a party organized by my son's school for host parents of international exchange students. The exchange student program has been a marvelous opportunity for young Americans to gain thought-provoking knowledge of our expansive world, while the foreign students have been fortunate to gain firsthand experience of American family life and democratic practices.

Some parents at that party were apprehensive about insurmountable cultural differences. Then the host said something I remember to this day: "No cultural differences can ever be as deep as the differences between a man and a woman." John Gray said it best: "Men are from Mars; women are from Venus."

Different does not mean inferior or unequal. Both men and women should be held in mutual esteem, which is a priori due any human being. Extreme feminism creates a dangerous precedent of vilifying men as a gender and ruining reputations based on allegations alone. It harms children, who are best served by living in a loving home of parental harmony and juxtaposition. Women and men are equally significant and splendidly dissimilar.

Let us not deprive future generations of fully experiencing the thrill of love's respectful pursuit or some good-humored flirting. Cassie Nightingale shows us how it ought to be done.

EPILOGUE

"The Unforgiving Minute"

One of my favorite poems of all times is "If" by Rudyard Kipling. It begins:

> If you can keep your head when all about you
> Are losing theirs and blaming it on you,
> If you can trust yourself when all men doubt you,
> But make allowance for their doubting too ...

And ends:

> If you can fill the unforgiving minute
> With sixty seconds' worth of distance run,
> Yours is the Earth and everything that's in it,
> And—which is more—you'll be a Man, my son!

I scribbled this booklet during the somber quarantine evenings and weekends of the 2020 spring, as an antidote to COVID-19 apprehension. Some of the stories were already ripe in my heart and just couldn't wait to be put down on paper. Others poured forth instantly. I wrote them for my son, my young sister, and the children of tomorrow.

May they "fill the unforgiving minute" with sixty seconds of courage, wisdom, and humanity, born from an independent mind and an unbreakable spirit!

CPSIA information can be obtained
at www.ICGtesting.com
Printed in the USA
LVHW050041280920
667253LV00002B/573